Here's a collection of poetry written b... confident, direct, far-ranging—a book ... to stare at the years gone by and at the pr... begins with a catalogue of blessings, with praise for poetry itself. The poet pledges her "allegiance to the natural world," her loyalty to that world, and all the things and the people that are part of that world. The book darkens, grows more complicated: what faith means, what love and family mean, what good luck means in a world of damage and danger—Joanne Esser takes it all on and gives us this thoughtful version of the world she pays such close attention to, for herself and her readers.

—Deborah Keenan
author of *The Saint of Everything*

Joanne Esser is able to find the words and the images that we struggle to conjure, from deep within, about silent longing and unspoken hope, about intricate currents of our nature, about appraised faith and interior blossoming. After reading this collection, I felt found and recognized. Esser's poetry sings in an easy, familiar cadence, a rhythm of the heart, of the heartland. The voices of children, their banter clear in the twilight as they play the old games, evoke the remembered sounds still echoing somewhere within oneself. This poetry and its voice will lead you to places you thought you had forgotten, and you will be quietly astonished.

—Lawrence Tjernell
editor at Longship Press

In *All We Can Do Is Name Them*, Joanne Esser sings of our innate fragility, our capacity for love and danger, and "what will remain." She writes of the feminine generational generosity of spirit. With an eye that captures the body of earth and also the body of the daughter, Esser is a poet of prayer, memory, and renewal. To read her is to find, for a moment, a place to rest.

—Lauren Davis
author of *Home Beneath the Church*

Joanne Esser's *All We Can Do Is Name Them* is as much a collection of prayers as it is a collection of poems. Blessings and invocations. Lamentations and litanies. From the ministrations of geese to deeply felt prayers of thanksgiving and especially of transformation, Esser celebrates the minuteness of our human lives while acknowledging all that can't be witnessed. "A poem is a room in which to pray," she tells us, and *All We Can Do Is Name Them* is a many-roomed house beckoning us inside.

—Denton Loving
author of *Crimes Against Birds* and *Tamp*

Joanne Esser's new book of poetry, *All We Can Do Is Name Them*, explores the world with deeply held joy. These generous poems ruminate about life, offering clarity and expansiveness. This is a book to come back to again and again. Esser's lovely, thoughtful poems offer us comfort and companionship.

—Mary Logue
author of *Heart Wood*

All We Can Do
Is Name Them

Joanne Esser

Fernwood
PRESS

All We Can Do Is Name Them

©2024 by Joanne Esser

Fernwood Press
Newberg, Oregon
www.fernwoodpress.com

Printed in the United States of America

Cover and page design: Mareesa Fawver Moss
Cover image copyright Jamie Heiden 2024
Author photo: Michael Gilligan www.michaelgilliganphotography.com

ISBN 978-1-59498-143-2

for my grandchildren,
and for all the children—
may their sense of wonder endure

CONTENTS

"But I don't believe
only to the edge
of what my eyes actually see
in the kindness of the morning,
do you?"
—*Mary Oliver, "The Pinewoods"*

Litany on an Autumn Late Afternoon

Bless the slow walkers of old, gray-muzzled dogs
and the quick ones with their sleek, young dogs
and the patient ones with rambunctious pups
they allow to take a dip in the lake.
Bless the new mothers pushing strollers,
cooing nonsense to their babies, tucking in
blankets as the breeze rises.
Bless the boy zooming along the path
on his orange bike who calls out
in his ten-year-old high-pitched voice, "On your left!"
as he swishes past the white-haired man pedaling.
Bless the gray woman in a wheelchair
and the young woman who pushes her along. Bless
both of their genuine smiles.
Bless the haloed girl riding on her daddy's shoulders
in slant sun, and bless that man who raises her up
to a place where she can see the world
lit up before her.
Bless the taut-bodied, rope-muscled runners
with their serious expressions,
and the thick-thighed, soft-bellied joggers
whose faces show even more courage.
Bless the whistlers, the hummers, and the ones
who choose to walk in silence.
Bless the loud, animated conversations between friends.
Bless the abandoned pacifier by the side of the path
and the child who is missing it.
Bless the teen in stars-and-stripes shorts
who rides his skateboard bare-chested,
his hat on backwards, not meeting anyone's gaze.
Bless the lovers, tall and short, old and young,
holding hands. Bless their unhurried pace.
Bless the breeze, its small hands that pluck
ready golden leaves, twirl them through the air
down onto the grass, onto the sidewalk, onto us.

Bless the chirps of the last crickets, the surprise
of wind chimes someone hung in a tree,
the hush of wind over water
and the buoys bobbing, now empty of their boats.

A Poem Is a Room

A poem is a room in which to pray—
a space empty enough to hold whatever
flows when you move away the boulders.

Here is the single window facing east,
the sturdy table and chair made by hand
from rubbed wood, the solid walls.

There's a hole cut in the floor
that opens to the soft green water
of your familiar pond.

Here you can gather what rises up
or what's just below the surface.
You can look down, unafraid of drowning,

dive in and reach for the flotsam
floating in your own veins. You can paint
this room any color, even hot pink,

even a color no one else likes. Who
are these words for, anyway? Will they
float out the window, stream to the top

of some mountain? Or burst into flame
when oxygen leaks in? If prayer is
what you're after, almost any words will work,

as long as they burn hot with the fuel
you know as truth. Then from every angle,
from a far distance, they can be read.

A poem is a safe house for words of that sheen,
even fragile, wind-ripped remnants.
They can still flap if you attach them fiercely to a post.

Brief Life

So many toads,
a huge hatching this summer.
Every step I take
startles them from their disguises
deep in damp grass.

They pop up
on strong, small legs
and hop—dash—bounce
fast across the trail
to a safer hiding place
just on the other side
so as not to be crushed
by my large feet.

How quick,
how short,
how precisely the stages
of their lives allow
them to grow,
how well-equipped
their brown bumpy bodies
for this pond and woods.

Nature keeps telling me
of brevity.
Then why am I surprised
when people get sick and die?

I think: it was too soon,
unfair. Yet who is to say
how long is long enough
for a life? I've had
sixty-one years already,
many leaps of luck,
getting out of the way just in time
too often to count.

The brief life of a woman
is relative, a gift of years,
not months or days.
Already a wealth,
though I no longer leap.

I stop to watch another toad,
no bigger than my toe,
pause on the edge of the path,
look around
with its huge, black-bead eyes.
I can see it breathing, its whole
leathery little body filling
and emptying, poised on the verge.

I am still,
not wanting to burden
this small being with fear.
How it studies the stalks of tall grass,
how it readies its muscled legs,
how it leaps without hesitation
into its perfect, ever-present brevity.

Momentary

Last night's
domed drop
on a fallen leaf
for a moment
reflects
infinity.

*

Seeing someone
by chance on the street,
someone you used to know,
perhaps loved:
pale ghost
made of loss,
memory of falling short,
the residue of all that trying.

*

The day long ago
when we skipped out
of Italian language class
to take a walk instead—
how it led us to the endless
field, sunflowers in every direction.
Countless golden brilliance
swallowed us whole
and we let it happen.

*

I don't trust time,
that it will deliver me
back to the moments I loved best.
Which is why I hold
an autumn leaf in my hands,
yesterday's supple red
now crumbling and curled,
the color of dried blood.

*

"One must mourn things daily,"
the poet said:
the sun gone down in the evening,
the moon extinguished
by the light of a new day
ending a perhaps perfect night.

We get used to endings,
barely notice when the good soup
is all eaten, the wine bottle empty.
There will be more; we have faith.

Yet sometimes people leave,
no way to contact them,
even if we wanted to.
In case we need again their particular scent,
the sound of their voice
on that singular evening when
we both saw, just for a moment,
the red flag on the stone tower
lit by moonlight
turn to flame.

Raspberries for Breakfast

It's already September, long past the time
when raspberries are at their peak.
I buy a pint anyway. I pay too much
but don't mind, in my greed
for the last remains of summer.

I must eat them right away. Even
in the cool dark of the refrigerator,
they will not keep long,
like the red morning sun
rising quickly over the horizon.

I pick one from my china bowl.
Silver drops of water cling
to its deep red hills and valleys.
In the first burst of sweetness,
I taste a premonition.

The juice carries in its dark syrup
a hint of its imminent demise,
the fuzzy gray rot of tomorrow
already built-in
to its aging sugars.

Yet when that overripe berry
melts on my tongue,
gives up its exquisite tang,
I swallow, too, a memory

of sun, those tangled branches
and poking thorns,
the smell of damp black soil
like a barely recalled love,

that dark-haired boy who ran
along the farm field paths.
He kissed me in the sultry heat
of a summer almost disappeared
from years ago, when I was young.

Red

At the edge of the caldera, flitting amidst
leafy brush, brown mud, cloud mist:

a sudden vermillion flycatcher.

It pauses on a branch, an exclamation
shouted out from the gray.

Why such red exuberance when
less brilliance would be enough?

Or consider the surprising drama
of the frigate bird's swollen balloon,

perfectly suited to advertise
to an interested female far away.

The ginger plant, too:

it bursts a small, lone flame
through eighty shades of Ecuadorian green.

Startling blazes of beauty in a place
few human eyes ever see.

They are not for us, these extraordinary
flashes. Sometimes the world just wants

to flaunt its own glamour, only a hint
of the fecundity swelling all around.

She Dreamed Long of Waters

Even when she was a young girl
she often woke remembering
the white tips of waves
as if all night she had been sailing
on choppy water. Sometimes
it was a calm lake she rode,
sometimes an entire ocean, always
ripples of silver sun across the surface.

She dreamed of waters she'd never seen
but always felt strangely at home there,
both above and below. Once
when she was in her twenties, she dove
deeper than ever before,
opened her eyes underwater to watch
fish drifting at her sides, staring at her,
puzzled to see a human in their midst—

green parrotfish with mouths like beaks,
yellow angels whose fins fanned open
like translucent wings, purple anemones
with soft waving tentacles. In the dream
she did not need air, did not even notice
she was without it, swam effortlessly,
felt deeply sad when she woke
in her own dry bed. She hated
to leave that hypnotic blue world,
that cool ease, the glide and hush of it.

Now she is older, having tromped heavily
on land for more years than she cares
to count. Her joints ache. Gravity
pulls her toward the core of the earth.
Her sleep is fitful now; she tosses under the sheets,
wakes easily. She rarely can hold onto
more than a fragment of any dream,
like wisps of tattered ribbon tugged
from dark into daylight. Still,

she carries those slippery nights
when it was easy to slide into
beckoning water, skin shining
in moonlight. She can conjure it,
distantly, like the simple melody
of a childhood song she once knew.

Signatures of the Invisible

Where Lake Superior meets land, secluded damp sand
smoothed, lit by August morning light, we
pull up our boats, careful not to disturb

the hieroglyphs laid down just before we arrived: tracks
of webbed gull feet, or terns, and delicate, tiny bird prints,
perhaps a piping plover who dug for worms on the beach,

small pads and toes of squirrel or mouse, and something
that dragged its tail, a long line snaking between
mammal paws—creatures long gone hours before we came,

hidden now in brush or grass on the hill above the beach,
or flown off to find breakfast—fish, crustacean, or
some deep green leaves. Just their signatures left here

in cursive loops, crisscrossing up and down the shoreline.
Unreadable script, though we try to decipher it,
regret our lack of mastery of languages other than our own,

accept that it's a design best viewed from above, a perspective
we can't have. Erased each day by wind and water,
this Etch-A-Sketch on which small beings write

each day anew in their skittery wanderings,
their searches and scratching, their morning routine
intersecting with that of all their neighbors,

and now with us, strangers, a foreign audience marveling
at the marks of their work, scribes mostly to the sky,
recording this precise place and time, this summer calm

before the gales arrive. What would it say, if it could be read?
*Sustenance is possible. The earth provides. Trust
in what you can find. The early bird gets the clam.*

Mysteries

The older I get, the more it seems right
to not know everything.
My curiosity about what happened
before the Big Bang has all but evaporated.

How this light got here all the way from the sun,
how the waves by the shore rise and
fall in such rhythm.
And I don't have to know the precise structure

of the coded strands of DNA entwined and floating
in each of your billions of cells
that make you the person you are,
sitting across from me at this wrought-iron table

by the edge of the water this afternoon.
It's enough to gaze at the symmetry,
to love the ancient and shimmering beauty
that makes up a face, this one and only face.

Reflections as Earth Realizes
That It Is Another Year Older

When Earth looks in the mirror lately, it notices how much it resembles
its parents.

Earth reluctantly made an appointment for a physical because it could
no longer ignore the recurring headaches, excessive thirst, and
unexplained fatigue.

Earth is sad when no one remembers to call and wish it a happy
birthday.

Earth believes wrinkles and scars are signs of character.

Earth feels frustrated always being third in line, but has accepted its
place.

Earth's hot flashes are keeping it from getting a good night's sleep.

Earth's many orifices ooze transparent blood.

It tickles Earth when small creatures burrow down into its soil.

Earth trembles when it has a panic attack.

Earth has found that tranquilizers no longer help.

Earth is comforted when Moon rocks its heavy waters back and forth,
back and forth.

Earth could spend hours each day playing with its pets.

Earth loves a good party.

Earth suffers from Fear Of Missing Out.

Earth is tired of all the ads that interrupt its favorite programs.

Earth is amused by the acrobatics of the animals swimming in its
oceans.

Earth never gets dizzy, no matter how many rides it goes on.

Earth admits it still gets choked up every time a baby is born.

Earth wishes it could take a day off without getting in trouble with the
boss.

Earth is looking forward to retirement.

One of Earth's favorite pastimes is to sit on the universe's front porch
and watch the asteroid show.

Some days Earth is overcome with emotion and is embarrassed by its
tears.

Earth reminisces about the good old days.

It is so noisy all the time now. Earth misses silence.

Allegiance

"The word tree and the word truth come from the same root."
—*Richard Powers*, The Overstory

On days of golden yellow leaves
sunlit against pure blue above,
walking beneath that singing canopy,
I think again of how love and luck
have found me, despite
my constant sense
that I am undeserving.
Of my unearned good fortune
and how easily it can be squandered.

What do I owe for long life, sturdiness,
being spared from much suffering,
everyone's birthright fear?

Though you may not understand
my obsessive appreciation for every
simple growing thing,
my foreknowledge of their brevity,
my awe of these trees, their ceaseless
reaching for endless sky, regardless,
I can't help it.
Life sung and then gone,
notes swallowed by the breeze—
and what will remain.

Allegiance to the natural world—
is it payment enough
for the debt of so much given?
Loyalty to all of it,
not just what's trapped
within or outside borders.
I am dedicated to these trees
that grow with disregard
for man-made regulations,

their roots spreading under soil,
unowned, unbound, blatantly ignoring
paperwork, passports, or prohibitions.

Their vast underground networks,
root hairs like brain fibers, synapses
sparking timeless knowledge
across acres, intelligence shared secretly
under our feet. One of the largest living creatures
on earth, great forests joined
in slow purpose, holding on beneath
what's visible, poised to outlive us all.

Doesn't reverence help? In the midst
of pain inflicted on too many beings,
intentional disregard for what's sacred,
the least I can do is pay attention,
proclaim a little of what I know is true,
listen for the whispers that hum
in one of the many languages
I don't know, the oldest wise words.

I touch the sturdy bark
of the grandmothers who have been living
long before our shouting and pillaging,
who will still rise from the soil after
we've all turned each other to ash.

Campout

It's a cold October night,
amber leaves above us turned to shadow,
and I'm in a tent
with my seven-year-old granddaughter.
We both smell
of campfire smoke: our hair,
our cozy fleece jackets. We zip
ourselves into our sleeping bags, all the way up.

It's her first time
sleeping outdoors and she asks
if we can keep one small flashlight on
for a nightlight, as if the thin beam
will keep us safe from the bears
she imagines clawing
the sides of the tent. It's alright
with me, whatever charm we invoke

to allow us both this dark night,
distant pinprick stars. *Tell me a story*,
she asks, and while I pause to think,
she embarks on one of her own,
this small but talkative girl—a tale
half-remembered, half-invented on the spot,
as dreams are, a story with rippled water
tumbling by, a wild expanse of sand,

her paddling a small, proud kayak
all by herself. She weaves the words
into a bold self-portrait, how she
navigated through wind and waves,
without any grown-up's help.
Once I also made myself the hero,
told stories about wandering
foreign cities alone, finding my way.

But after all these lucky years
of living, I know I've never had
a real test. It's easy to be brave
when you're given so much good:
a little girl who holds your hand
as she falls asleep, who trusts you
completely in the safe Minnesota dark.

"Everything that can wreck a life
has been done before,
done to you, even. That's all
inside you now."

—*Barbara Kingsolver, "How To Have A Child"*

Finality

To finally know autumn,
inhale rusty smoke-scent.
See the last
of the leaves
battered by cold
rain, the gorgeous
brutal scattering.
What was bright
is leaving us. Yet
we are still here, watching.

Enormity

Begin with a single grain of sand
on a beach next to a vast ocean.
Maybe you are one of those grains.

Telescope out slowly.
Pan wide from above.
First the edge of the shore,
the water stretching out for miles.

Pull back; see a whole country,
a continent floating in blue.
Then farther out still, only
small bits of land, brown, tan,
flecks of green, fading
to gray against all the seas,
the clouds, the sphere of earth
now like a child's swirled marble.

Keep moving away slowly until
the planet itself is but
a sand-grain speck in an endless
sky, dark, dotted with jeweled stars,
moons, cycling, rotating among
perhaps many worlds,

a universe, or universes
unimaginable within
my small brain, my
sand-grain scale
self. There I am
down below
nearly invisible,

a speck that fits snugly into
the grand design
but not a critical piece.

My choices (for better
and for worse), my gestures
and offerings, my mistaken attempts
only miniscule blips
in the functioning of
a doomed planet. My daily
waking, walking, working
like an industrious ant, but smaller
on the floor of an impossibly huge forest.
My tragedies only tiny hiccups.

It lets me off the hook. I squirm
and thrash, I bluster and fret
and everything keeps going
the way it will.

Even the best of us
only moves against other
sand grains, rubbing futilely
until we are washed
into the great ocean.

Lines That Come at One a.m.
on the Eve of Trump's Inauguration

According to the laws here, you can't cross the street.

The sidewalk is too fragile to walk on
with both feet at the same time.

And no one will show you the black rug where the decisions are made.

The firing squad has already tossed something into the crowd.

Fragments fall like snowflakes.
You try to catch one, but you can't,
even though you're wearing your best mittens.

A story you heard on the news that was important, something
about a woman and her lost baby, has slipped out of your reach.

Outside the window, twilight is caught in the trees.

The road out of town diminishes into one-point perspective.

You squint your eyes to watch
as a parade marches by.

Music plays from a hidden speaker.

It's a great day for omens.

Before you know it, invisibility becomes a habit.

From Disaster to Chimpanzees

Scrolling through headlines
before I go babysit my grandchildren,
I stumble into familiar sinkholes.

If only we could juggle one moment
of disaster at a time,
if bad news came in droplets
that slowly slide down
the window glass rather than
torrents of driving rain.

Perceived all at once, it's unbearable:
climate change truth, the string of lies
belching from leaders' mouths,
one more cage of brown-skinned children,
another blood-spattered classroom.

At bedtime my granddaughter shows me
a song she wrote
about moving up to first grade—
her words spelled like they sound,
a melody that changes
each time she sings it:
"huray kindrgardn is ovr and
i will go to first grad i m happy
for sumr when I can do watevr
I want."

What does she see in her
six-year-old version of hope?
Not melting glaciers, dying birds,
not guns in the hands of teenagers.
She sees her young teacher
who will tell her stories.
She sees dancing numbers,
letters lining up magically before her eyes
and she beams, "I can read this, Grandma!"

I sit on her bed as she tells me
all about chimpanzees, facts she has learned
from her kindergarten research project.
How they use sticks
to poke anthills and patiently wait
for the ants to climb on the sticks,
then scoop them up to their mouths.
(*But they don't eat the sticks, Grandma.*)
How clever those chimpanzees,
with hands just like ours, except
with longer fingers, perfectly adapted
for swinging through green jungle trees.

I tell her that apes are the closest
animals to humans, problem-solvers
who devise tools, use their brains
like we can. I'm not sure if she
believes me, but she wishes
she could have a chimpanzee for a pet.
It could swing in the backyard with her,
if only it didn't get so cold here
in the winter. *They have to live
where it's warm, Grandma*, she knows.

I rub her back, think of chimpanzees,
green leaves and humid jungles,
summer and the chance
to *do whatever I want*, song lyrics
in six-year-old capital letters,
the word *huray*, as the drizzle begins
outside her bedroom window.

I think of the children
behind the iron bars—
what songs will they invent
that are strong enough to hold
their too-early knowledge
of what it means to be taken,
locked up and left?

I whisper to my granddaughter
as she curls into the covers,
rain now pelting the glass,
*And chimpanzees take good care
of their babies.*

Migrant Detention Camp:
Fragments

Last night I dreamed of drowning kittens.
Someone had thrown them
into a churning sea.
Even as they mewed
and pawed at the waves,
they were slipping under the surface.
I knew they wouldn't make it.

Aren't we all witnesses?
I see their faces
in the newspaper, on my screen,
twenty-four hours a day.
I don't want to see them.
I can't not see them.

I plant sunflowers in the black soil
of my garden while
bodies huddle on a cement floor.

The bloodred sun sizzles
on desert horizon.

Can they see birds out the window?
Are there any windows?

The body does not get used to it—
the emptiness of arms,
the sound of children's cries.

Can they remember what birdsong sounds like?

Even packed into a crowded room,
this is the most profound loneliness:
The waiting. The not knowing.
The missing.
The shameful turning away
of anyone passing by. No one out here
willing to look them in the eye.

We thought that maybe time would fix it—
everything gets better eventually,
every violence comes to an end,
doesn't it?—
but all we have is the present,
where it is still happening.

There are a few patchy wildflowers
pushing out through the cracks.
We name them after what we
have failed to be: Desert Hopeflower,
Blazing Star of Safety, Justice's Paintbrush,
Common-Decency Weed.

What happens to the body
when there are no more tears,
when everything wet has evaporated
and the throat is too parched
even to cry out?

Some will stand stone still,
all the spark fizzled out.
Some will lie down
and ache for sleep. Some
will not bother getting up again.

There must be worlds
where the sun does not shrivel
the sweet bodies of children
until they dry up and drop.

One day someone will find
written in a large book
that smells of mildew
the tragedy of our ignorance.

Lockdown Drill

In my neighborhood when I was a girl,
we'd spend long summer days hidden
beneath the bridal veil, the lilacs,
the bushes that grew round red berries—
our secret hideout, place of sweet
blossom smells, small-leafed branches like a roof,
walls of green, dense shadows for protection.

All day we'd crouch, spying on whatever
went past on the sidewalk—John the Mailman,
Mr. Meisner gardening next door, the pregnant
lady from the apartments pushing a stroller,
the fat beagle on a leash—but they didn't see us.

We'd pick red poison berries, grind them up
with rocks, add some puddle water and dirt
to make a potion we could feed to the bad guys.
We knew they'd die from it, and we'd be safe.

Today when the announcement comes,
I gather all the children, sit in the dark
behind a locked door at the bottom of the stairs,
try to keep everyone quiet and pretend
we're hiding. *It's only a practice*, I whisper.

The children are confused.
Though only four years old, they know
more than we think they do
about bad things that can happen in a school.
They've heard (even if we try to keep it
from them) about men with guns,
boys with guns. I must shush their questions
for long minutes until we get the all-clear.

As I sit cross-legged on the rug, holding
one's small hand, another child curled on my lap,
I remember those girlhood days,
how we schemed for hours in our backyards,

in charge of the world behind the hedges
until our mothers opened doors that were
never locked and called us in for lunch.
Danger was only a game we could choose to play.

Magician's Assistant

Even when you know it's an illusion,
it's nerve-wracking to watch
your daughter get sawn in half.
Tied by wrist, ankle, and neck
with ropes, she enters a coffin-sized
wooden box, each rope then pulled out
through holes and knotted there.
One by one the magician slides
panes of glass, sheets of steel
straight through slits in the box, and finally,
a jagged saw slices back and forth
with a terrible grating sound
where her abdomen would be.
You are her mother, so you can't help
but picture every wound, every
potential fate: someone taking her,
tying her up, beating her,
leaving her for dead.
In those long minutes as the blade rips
through wood and real sawdust scatters,
fear of everything you've ever imagined
that might hurt your daughter runs frantic.
You know it is make-believe, designed
to fool the audience, yet your mother-mind
travels to all the places—
bedrooms, alleys, basements, cold
vacant lots—where things happen to
lovely girls. Yet when the magician
unlocks the clasps, opens the heavy lid,
there she is, alive. He cuts the ropes
that bind her and she sits up, smiling
in her black Victorian lace and
lets the audience know she is fine,
not a scratch. You breathe then
and realize you've been
holding your breath all this time,
waiting for the proof.

The Mothers

Here are the mothers. They are busy
laying cool cloths on fevered foreheads;

they stir thick soup in pots on the fire,
open windows, sweep out the dust,
rock to calm tiny, desolate hearts.

They do worry when they hear the news.
What's this good world coming to? they think.

But they can't afford despair.
There is too much to be done.

They sleep when they can, lightly, listening,
and wake again with the first light

to mend all that's torn, glue all that's broken,
piece together warmth from scraps.

They speak with their hands,
not to crowds, not with microphones,
but with strokes of children's hair.

Can you see all their faces? Under veils or
under make-up, beneath lines worn
by time, so many mirrors of god.

What I Can See

1. The doctor recommends
   zapping just one eye,
   whichever one I prefer,
   to make it sharp enough again.

2. Their boots sink in, up to their thighs;
   undaunted, the children march
   across the playground, lifting
   knees high.

3. White spray obscures
   his features as he rides
   a wave, belly to the sea.
   But I know that grin
   behind the droplets.

4. I'll admit it: I've forgotten
   many things.

5. Two Canada geese
   tread a half-frozen pond
   as delicately as they can
   with such large black feet.

6. From here,
   I can't tell which bundle of wool
   is which—only
   bright pink, turquoise,
   purple against
   brilliant white snow.

7. In the backyard, rotting gray
   fence boards lean
   like drunken soldiers
   as the man I used to trust
   tries to explain again.

8. The eye not chosen
   will be left alone
   so that it can be counted on
   for reading poetry.

9. No face in the window any more,
   then no window,
   then no train.
   Only the shivering
   maples letting go
   of yellow leaves one
   at a time.

10. I will never stop seeing
    those rickety gray spikes.

11. It makes me happy that,
    though the geese could fly away,
    they have found a way
    not to fall through.

All We Do Not Know
about Each Other

I lived with her day in and day out
for decades, saw her every morning
fresh and smiling, packing our lunches,

heard her on the phone, watched her
make grocery lists, to-do lists
for committees, Christian Mothers,

Community League, for bake sales,
fish fries, holiday fairs, raising money
for this charity or that, and yet

when I glimpsed her alone at the end
of the day, kneeling by her bed,
I couldn't know what sorrows

she carried, what memories from before
she was my mother were locked away.
What she prayed. What she dreamed.

She was not the kind of person
to tell of her dreams in the morning.
Or to give voice to worry, fear.

And me, all I've kept hidden,
not told my children or my husband.
The tiny bits of indescribable history

we carry like a million-piece puzzle,
flashes of color, shape, scattered hints,
but no one sees the assembled picture,

not even ourselves. We're strangers, always—
though we share bread and lie close,
though our habits are familiar.

Even when we touch, skin to skin,
a layer shields our salty essence,
our invisible fog, breath in and out,

all that cannot be witnessed. Then
one day, when our beloved
does something surprising,

"out of character," how shocked
we are. The impulse must have been there
all along, moving like a spark

through their blood, and we never
saw it, never felt it, even when
we slept curled around their body.

Mending

My mother darned socks in the evening
while the television droned on and my father
sat behind his newspaper. Reading glasses
on her nose, her hands worked quick and sure,

an egg-shaped wooden bulb stuck in the toe
or heel as she stitched holes closed.
She sewed patches on the knees of our corduroys
and later, on our jeans, until we grew

too embarrassed to let her. Though we could afford
to buy new socks, new pants or shirts, she
insisted on replacing lost buttons, stitching all
our torn seams. Why pay for something new

if it could be fixed? She kept her sewing box
close to her chair, the many compartments
for small scissors, a rainbow of spools and floss,
needles sized for every separate purpose.

No words as she worked, just pushing the needle
with practiced fingers through fabric stiff or silky.
My mother never gushed endearments, rarely told us
that she loved us, didn't call us pet names.

She rarely scooped us up for hugs or snuggled
with us on the davenport. But she also never allowed
us to run off with a toe poking through our sock
or a hole where our heel could rub against our sneakers.

Later after she was gone and so many things got torn—
my confidence, my marriage, my house, my heart—
I realized that I never learned how to mend
and it's too late now to ask her.

Headline

Somewhere in the bitter January cold of this St. Paul night
is the mother, just minutes after she's made the decision
to wrap her newborn infant, still wet with afterbirth,
umbilical cord clamped with a binder clip, and carry him
under cover of dark to the cathedral. I can see her,
alone, walking out into below-zero wind,
shivering, maybe bleeding, opening
the heavy doors, entering the church's dim hollow.
She places her baby in a plastic laundry basket.
She chooses a spot where someone will find
her child. Someone who would know what to do.

When she sets that basket down, does she cry?
Does she tremble, or set her face like stone?
What does it feel like to tear yourself
away from a wriggling, whimpering being
that emerged from your own body?
Does she fill her empty spaces with the imagined face
of a good person stepping into that shadowed church,
scooping up the child? Does she imagine some kind arms?
What goodness and kindness has she ever known?

The story is not new. Back in the twelfth century,
nuns attached boxes to the convent gates
for abandoned babies, *foundling wheels*.
A choice: instead of throwing it into the Tiber,
a mother could deliver her baby
anonymously to the care of nuns.
In the new millennium, the boxes have returned,
insulated now, modern cradles on the fences
with built-in alarms to call the sisters, who phone
the hospital to pick up the baby within minutes.
Suffering, fear of the authorities
remain, as ever. But here at least,
the child will be safe.

The newspaper says a janitor found the infant
minutes after she left him, called paramedics
and the priest, who baptized the baby and named him.

The child will be fine, a healthy boy;
the news article a guarantee that someone
with an ache of their own
will take him, raise him as their son.

But where does she go afterward,
that woman whose body throbs
with eternal residue? After she slips
quietly back into the frozen dark,
her story won't make it into the headlines.

"What is confusion anyway, except a mystery
for which someone thinks there should be a solution?"
—*Jim Moore, "At Fifty, #9"*

Portrait with White Space

For Pearl

She is comfortable
living in the white space
between certainties.
There are no guarantees,
she knows, and she finds
this interesting.

She has learned to yield
to what will be
with grace, finds
comfort in the turning
of seasons, the cycles
of the plants and the animals
and of the self;

she delights in the leaf
only half-changed,
midway between green and the startling
fire-orange it is destined to become.

She has discovered
that no one knows any real answers,
or, rather, there are a multitude
of answers, so we're on our own,
lost and stumbling but reaching.

She loves paradox and sees
beauty in shades of gray.
The empty space between the words, the
implications between the lines, all
that is not said but is implied,
the hidden layers beneath the street
that go all the way down to the core
are her terrain, a huntress
of meaning, walking right through
the mystery.

"If this is all I can have," she says, "then
this is what I will take.
Uncertainty is not so bad a thing
to live in, as long as one can find a warm spot.

It's fairly simple:
I will know when my life is going
the direction it is supposed to go
when it goes that way.

All the beautiful stuff out the window
is enough, if only
I can find a way out into
its perfume and flutter.

When you ask me
all these questions, I don't know
if my replies will be the ones
you expected, or the same ones I will give
tomorrow, but I'll tell you
what I think right now:

There's a lot of essential
wisdom barely concealed
between the lines of type
on the page, under the lines
etched on faces, below the lines painted
on the roadway, so that's
where I'm looking.

There's something eternal about the way
my children's hair glows
when the sunlight streams into
their bedroom windows, so I don't
pull the shades. I let it all come in."

Rainy Day

The rain began to fall the morning after
he left. It kept falling all day, so fine
she could barely see it falling
unless she looked against the red brick
of the house next door, or the black of
the apple tree. It swept too soft
to plink or splatter, a constant hush,
a sound you could mistake for a summer breeze.
Her freshly washed clothes hanging on the line
soaked in the rain all day.
She read poems, wrote a letter
that needed to be written,
watched the invisible falling.
In the afternoon she went upstairs,
heated a bowl of leftover soup,
its mild onions, chunks of tomato, and beans
fragrant in red broth, exactly what she needed.
The rain kept on, straight down
like something delicate crushed into a dust
too small to see, impossible to gather.
It whispers its hopeless benediction—
what is lost what is lost what is lost what is—
as she stays there at the window, watching.

Old Letters

"I am struggling," I write,
"to find as much meaning in the present
as I attribute to the past."

A paragraph at least, detailing
the anguish of my labors
here, alone.

And he will reply,
"The light is beautiful in the afternoon
here in Stockholm. I am
missing you more every day."

As if the longing itself
was an essential element
of what we came here to find.

Am I in love with his sadness?
—that which feels so familiar, as if
I have always known it.

There is something in both of us
that hungers for melancholy,
the way it shadows the chair,
the wine glass, the vase of flowers
fresh from the market, creates
the illusion of depth.

How we prefer dusk
to rising morning,
the memory of a thing almost
more than the thing itself.

We can shape it then,
in our hands, in our words,
the past always more pliable
than the present, with its
tendency toward chilling winds,
sour smells, the feel of hard surfaces.

What will happen when I throw away
the letters, the only physical evidence
that links memory to the tangible world?

There will be no proof
that what we once had
ever existed, except
deep in the secret beating
of our twin hearts.

"If you
unfold an origami swan, and flatten the
paper, is the paper sad because it has
seen the shape of the swan, or does
it aspire toward flatness, a life without
creases?"

—Victoria Chang, "The Clock"

Rejecting Longing

I page through piles of old poems
in which I am walking alone on cobbled streets
or watching a train leave the station,

someone I thought I knew carried away.
How I dwelled in illusion, mistaking
conjured gestures for nourishment of the heart.

Longing itself is a kind of food,
a sugar I crave and have often indulged,
though it always leaves me hungry.

Now that I am tired and growing older
I finally begin to see love
as substance, and plain; how it is built

stone on top of stone in the daily-ness
of showing up, its smells and dust,
its weary yawns and warmed leftovers.

I look up at the stars and they are not there.
I see the memory of what they once were,
transmitted down to me over time,

not enough light to read by.
Beauty to admire but not make use of.
Like past loves, too far away to touch.

This is the riddle of my life:
whether to examine the real—
what's simple and gritty, fleeting,

what will one day inevitably be gone—
or to live in the cloud of desire,
insubstantial and shimmering,

trading one for the other.
Always asking, "Is there more?"
and, while looking up,
risk missing what is in front of me.

One of the First Days

"...Can you know, when you're not even
a bud, but poised at some brink?"
      —Mark Doty, "Verge"

Can they tell? The cook and the girl who takes
our drink order? As we sit on the nearly deserted
patio under an umbrella where no one

with any sense would sit, waiting for the end
of the silver drizzle that was not predicted,
we sip our beers, uncertain of what to say.

It's cold and we are new to this, pulling from
inside our warm throats barely enough words
to keep fueling the exchange. I'm wondering

whether you are as miserable as you look,
the waterfall splashing over the rock face
in the distance, just above your shoulder.

You propose a hike, something I usually
enjoy, but today I am dressed all wrong
and I know the trails will be muddy.

Yet there is some small charge here,
an exchange, barely tangible,
that makes me bold, so I agree.

Neither of us can tell where this will lead
even as we set off, hoods up against the rain,
trudging almost dutifully, sticking with

the plan, despite the change in the sky,
all that gray. We follow the creek, its rush
winding through woods until we get in deep.

In the silence, ease comes. A synchronized pace.
Can anyone see in the damp of our skin
its shine? What is just starting to become true?

As we walk in a rhythm, ignoring now the wet,
there is a quick sound. We hear it at the same
time, stop in our tracks, shoulders almost touching.

A single bird song pierces from somewhere
through the rain. Invisible. Sharp. Strong.
We can't identify the call. Not yet. But

years from now, we will remember
that sound, the way we both studied
the trees, searching eagerly for its source.

The Benefits of Anonymity

Each sparrow, to humans
from a distance looks indistinguishable.
Their morning noises blend

like an old-time brass band
tuning up.

When I walk on the path near the lake
I veer for a moment or two
to the edge. I am there, on the water,

wavery, a dim shape floating
on the surface. It looks like me
but it's not.

To see myself is nearly impossible,
trapped as I am inside
this thin but impermeable skin.

So many people make a crowd,
even when we're all enclosed
in our separate cars,
windows rolled up in the heat,
lined up and jammed on the highway
in rageful slow motion.
We prefer speed.

Yet it's slowness that gives us enough
time to catch glimpses of what lands
on the apple tree branch,

its feathers not simply brown.
If I watch long enough, I can tell
when the note is about to be released.

I can see the flecks of gold
and pure white speckled
into its shadows.

If I had enough mirrors
arranged at certain angles
and I waited until
morning seeped into my dreams,

perhaps I could recognize
another side of myself,
one I'm having trouble remembering.

If I turned off the radio
with its endless litany of pain,
maybe I could take off these boots
that weight me to the ground,

rise up high enough to see
what's always been under my feet.
Or rest on a branch,

only one of many hundred
sparrows opening my beak,
making my brassy noise.

Self-Help

At the table by the window on a late Sunday afternoon,
three young women, college-age, are animated,
their voices high, flat Midwestern vowels loud over their coffee.

One is expounding about a book they have all apparently
read, a club, it seems, and she explains (her voice going up
at the end of her sentences like she's seeking agreement?)

how the subconscious works. About *Joy* with a capital J,
how the mind draws to it what it needs. She quotes now and then,
reading in her nasal voice passages about meditation,

manifesting destiny. This young woman seems to be
the leader, her voice fast, barely pausing for breath.
Pursuing our goals, she says, in a blue-and-white striped sweater,

heavy silver necklace. *Oh totally*, one agrees. Their long
straight hair, all styled the same, is part of the uniform
for pretty, educated, upper-middle-class, white young women

seeking peace between the pages of a paperback
over caramel lattes. About self-acceptance, *like . . . you're okay*,
the power of affirmation. *Say it out loud*, the leader commands.

"I am brilliant, bright, and beautiful!" She may not
notice, in her eagerness to explain each point, but
this entire world is already designed to affirm them.

"I'm going to appreciate how special I am," she recites
to her three friends safe at a coffee shop at a moment
on a February Sunday in the youth of their lucky lives.

Revision

The trouble with the present is
it's a lot of work.

You have to keep redoing it,
every day a rewrite

in the face of new plot twists
that insert themselves, unbidden,

into the narrative you had planned.
Not like the past, a well-plotted novel

that always ends the same way
no matter how many times you reread it.

But *now*, you never get to the ending.
You can't be sure the good people win,

that anyone is safe, or that love
can be counted on to last.

You have to come back to the desk
every day, pen poised to give order to

complications galore, the dizzying array
of windblown fates and intentions

that have been swept out of the blue
into your doorway today.

Portrait of Mike at Fifty-Two

His favorite word lately is *aspirational*.
(He impresses all the construction guys
at work whenever he uses it.)

He bought brand-new aspirational shorts
that will fit just right when he loses
a couple of pounds.

And his aspirational garage sits out back
half-built for the past year as he
adjusts here, revises plans there,
attends to every small detail.

He wakes at five each morning to go
to a thankless job in hopes it will lead
to what he really wants—
if only he knew what that might be.

But not before he goes to the gym,
lifts his weights, a bit more each day.
(Only this morning he achieved
a temporary personal best.)

Tomorrow we'll rent a camper-van
and drive across hundreds of miles
to jagged mountains and red-rock canyons
where we've never been before.

He will study all the maps,
select the trails with sheer drop-offs
that lead up to exceptional views.

His heart will soar as we steadfastly hike
endless narrow paths. The sweat
will feel so sweet as he aspires

to the very highest point,
leaving the rest of the world far below.

Perplexities

1. How a bullet can come through a window,
   land in the dog's water dish
   just beside the man standing in the kitchen.
   On the news they said it seemed to come from nowhere;
   amazingly, it touched no one on the way.

2. In only one generation,
   the wings of the swallows who live near the highway
   have shortened, to make their flight more precise,
   so they can swerve quickly, to avoid fast traffic.
   The survivors pass along their secrets.

3. All week, the rain's
   litany of sadnesses drums on my roof.
   How it keeps pouring; the creek rushes,
   rises up over its banks, washes out the road.
   I stay dry inside.

4. Though thousands of asteroids
   zoom through space and our telescopes
   watch for close calls, not one
   has collided with Earth in quite a while.
   We rely on sheer luck.

5. The way orphaned girls in a country
   across the sea have taught themselves
   to sing together unaccompanied and teach
   the young ones perfect harmony
   made of loneliness and truth.

6. How two strangers' eyes meet
   on a crowded train and each recognizes
   something familiar in the other, and
   they get to choose whether or not
   to speak of it, or forever pass up the chance.

7. How the rain eventually stopped.
   How it always does. How there is so much
   to clean up after everything slowly dries out
   and we can see what is salvageable
   and what is lost.

Morning in Minneapolis

It was a long night
filled with haunted dreams
of running, sirens, streets
erupting, rumbling turned
to flames, fire seeking ruin,
making way for something
new. In the burning
I saw familiar shadows,
the incessant flickering
that has been with us
from the beginning. Looming
larger than our bodies, shadows
made of fear and privilege
take up so much space.

I tell myself: Wake up. It's
an old story. From the ashes, they say,
a bird can be reborn. But how
does it learn to fly?
Crawling out from under
broken beams, piles of rubble,
it claws its way into sunlight.
Morning on Lake Street—
the night's rage spent.
All around, crumbled remains
of what could no longer stand.

Daylight comes no matter what
happened last night. I am
still here, not entirely consumed
by my illusions, by guilt. Now
I must ask: What comes next?
Baby steps out of so-easy silence.
Speak one word, then two, then
more—not only to pray. Can I learn
a new language? Discern what words
are necessary? Know
that I don't know.

I awaken to my ignorance,
the proof of what is broken,
has broken the necks
of too many to count.
I begin to count them.
It doesn't change
anything. Except for
me.

I take a step out from behind
my window box, my full, scented
peonies dropping their pink
petals on our sidewalk. Morning
in Minneapolis, my city. No one
is exempt. I can't afford to fall
back to sleep.

Prayers

I recite a litany of praise
and a list of pleas, like spells
against gathering clouds

doubting that they will reach you,
even as I voice them, in your
distant apparent indifference.

Language always falls short.
We are on our own here,
and we are fucking it up.

Whatever holy spark started it all
we have claimed as our own,
grabbed to hold and to keep,

and in our greed, crushed
the delicate breath from what
it was meant to be.

Still, there are elements
we cannot ruin: the sun,
which carries on, out of our reach,

and the moon, with her power,
her undeniable rhythms.
If there is a response

to the hollow echoes of prayers,
it is this: how breath can calm fear,
how the light returns in the morning.

Hike to Rattlesnake Ledge

Leave the city, your daughter behind
the wheel, bumper to bumper with all
the driven people chugging to their high-
rise cubicles. Veer away toward the blue
mountains you can barely see in the bright
haze of May. Roll down the window
just a crack. Weave up the winding road
past Douglas firs. Ascend to the unmarked
entrance between trees. Park the car,
gather water bottles, granola bars, sunglasses,
the jacket you will wear only for the first
ten minutes, then shed. Follow your daughter
to the trailhead where she has walked
many times before.

This is her place. Let her lead.
Take it step by step, climbing steeply
as you talk. Don't be afraid to admit
your need to stop, drink some water.
Your legs will feel the work and respond.
Let your words rise up on cool drafts
of mountain air, crystalline. Heavy thoughts
released here will lift, be lighter to carry.
Face forward as you hike, brave enough
to approach questions you've never asked
aloud before. Pass slower hikers on the trail.
Let other hikers, young, eager, pass you.
Round the final curve, a switchback that
permits you to stand at last on the ledge.
What you've come all this way for.

Stand among the granite boulders high above
the valley, up at the tops of trees and look
out to the blue that goes on forever. Then
behold your daughter standing next to you:
the curious child she once was, the uncertain
adolescent, all the ages she has been, telescoped into
this strong woman who has brought you here.

My Friend Argues for the Superiority of Russian as a Better Language for Poets

On the Moscow subway in the late '90s,
men in black wool coats read paperbacks
of poetry, Pushkin, Tolstoy, Yevtushenko,
savoring the collective grief
they all recognize, words that lend themselves
more easily to the sigh of universal need.

One word means ten different things,
a gulp of built-in metaphor understood
even by Russian school children,
that makes breakfast conversation into poetry.
Doesn't everything stand for something else?
Add the cynical tone, dark humor like crumbs
of black bread left on the table, the same as it's been
for hundreds of years.

Imagine if a single English word
could conjure so much in one stroke.
Take *fog*, for instance: at first, the literal
damp gray weather; but what if it was also
a kind of soup simmered all day
by grandmothers, and, too, a wanderer
lost in northern Minnesota woods,
and a kind of hat to shade the sun,
a fizzy drink, a poison mushroom, the act
of coughing, and the exact moment
the soul leaves the body.
So much leaping in every mind
with the utterance of just one word!

But look at the fat Oxford dictionary:
too many words, all naming a nuance
that's a shade unlike the next. Embarrassment
of choices, like the overflowing shelves
in the grocery store, a hundred kinds of cereal alone,
that makes my Russian friend dizzy to see.

No clarity in sparseness here, on our street
of tall houses, green lawns, carefully planted gardens.
But then, we've rarely shared helplessness,
a spare vocabulary behind closed doors,
fear of being heard. No recent wars
on our soil, our backyards never threatened
with blast, no common shared despair—
at least not yet, not in our neighborhood.

This language is my only tool.
I wander down the cluttered aisles,
search for precise unwieldy words
to stake my claim in the decade's unfolding,
always wishing for something
more compact, like a three-room apartment
we could all cram in, play music, and see
the same sky through the one tiny window.

Do the Gods See Us

When the gods look down,
do they see us humans
like a pile of fallen leaves,
strewn in thick layers over the ground,

anonymous, mostly drab
shades of brown, now and then
a still-tender yellow,
a single red that has held its bright?

Do they nod, seeing how it plays out again,
the cycle of effort, then letting go,
twirling down, piling up,
dead ones blowing around,
all crumbling to dust?

No individual leaves visible
from that distance, only
the accumulated scum of what once was.

Do they wait patiently for the new buds
of spring, the starting over
that they know will eventually happen?

"A deer rises onto her haunches
to reach for an apple,

though many fallen apples are on the ground."

—*Jane Hirshfield, "A Ream Of Paper"*

Faith

*"It's strange to lose a thing the size of a god
but not his blessings."*
     —Max Garland, "Keep In Touch"

I used to believe in heaven.
Now I believe in rest,
a peaceful ceasing
of the striving.

Whatever mountains I summited,
I summited. I saw the view.
Whichever ones I tried to climb
and quit, I quit. It doesn't matter.

My father believed in hard work.
No excuses. And his own rightness.
His life was proof of that:
visible rewards for all his efforts.
Certainty of more to come.
I was always small next to that.

At the end of each day,
my mother would kneel
in her nightgown next to her bed,
hands folded. I don't know
what words she prayed. I imagine
she asked for help, and for
forgiveness for everything
she failed to get right.

The saints listened. She counted on it.
Bestowed protection, intercession,
powers she lacked. Kept her children
healthy. (The ones that survived.)

From my mother's drawers after she died,
I resurrected her gloves in slender boxes,
a lace veil she wore to church
in the old days. A rosary in a velvet pouch.

I kept them, keep them still.
Though I don't believe in
the things that were for her a raft
in turbulent seas, I believe
in what she instinctively gave me.
The unearned blessings.
The luck of this life.

May Crowning

Boys and girls lined up in obedient rows
in the courtyard near the convent
for the ceremony every spring,

released from our pencil-lead classrooms,
me in my plaid uniform skirt, sun-warmed,
scent of lilacs blessing the air.

How I longed to be the girl
chosen to carry the crown of flowers,
to walk down the aisle past the rest

of us children squirming in our too-tight
collars; she would walk slowly,
reverently toward the statue of the Virgin Mary.

As the rest of us sang in our innocent voices
to Our Lady (my voice timid, though I loved
those hymns), that girl, honored above all,

would climb the stepladder
to reach up, place the crown firmly
on Mary's head. She would not

stumble; they never chose a clumsy girl.
What would be her secret? How did an ordinary
schoolgirl manage such poise?

Each year I would pray my hardest
that a beam of heavenly light
would shine down directly on my head,

an unmistakable sign that I was
Divinely Chosen. The nuns would recognize
immediately that I was the rightful one

and rush to hand me the flower crown
in front of the whole school.
Instead, I watched with envy

(perhaps my greatest childhood sin),
as the perfect girl fulfilled her role perfectly,
her long blond hair gleaming in the sun,
her saddle shoes steady as she
rose on tiptoes to place the beautiful
crown of flowers exactly centered

on Mary's smooth head.

Making Do

She wanted a dog,
but they gave her gerbils.

Two of them, in a wire cage.
She named them
Peanut and Marshmallow.

You could hold them,
but not for long.
They'd squirm to get away.
And they couldn't sit on your lap.

It was a virtue, then,
settling for almost
what you wanted.
It prevented you
from seeming greedy.

When they asked you
if you were happy
with your gift,
the right answer was
to smile quietly
and nod.

Kick the Can

Those summer nights as magical as myths:
the way we waited for it to get dark enough,
how we wore black t-shirts to make us invisible
when we hid behind bushes, around the corners
of neighbors' houses, never sure which shadow-shape
was who. How our blood felt like jazz, that adrenaline
surge when we saw a chance to make a break,
run full-out before the one who was It
could yell out our names. There was triumph
in the sound of a tin can being booted
across the lawns, a spark of daring
to free our trapped comrades, bravado
that we somehow already knew was finite.

Pour it on, use it up, spend those hours
of speeding childhood, pre-adolescent energy
like a violet-hot force that made us
glow in the dark, those nights when all we needed
were our friends and some guts and
a wicked sense of humor and we could
hold onto each other for Dear Life, could
chase, push, tackle, call each other
by nicknames that stuck: J-socks, Rock,
Juddly, making it up as we went along.
There was a complicated list of rules, and
as long as we all agreed, it was sweet, sweet
smells of cut grass, kid sweat, as we rolled
in summer that stained our knees and clung
to our hair, scented our skin, bodies
tumbling and shining with it,
until the moon grew bright, the stars rose
above our houses and our moms
wanted us home, until the next night
when the crew would gather again
to feel a kind of ecstasy that was only possible
for those few summers of our lives.

Snow Day

When we were little, Brother, we'd spin
in circles in the living room until
we fell down dizzy with laughter,
arms and legs tangled together

in circles in the living room and
outside our window, snow piled up.
Our arms and legs tangled into snowsuits,
boots, wool across our faces, bundled

to run out headlong into snow, piled up
in soft curves. We threw our bodies,
bundled, with wool across our faces
fearless into the cold, sparkling with delight.

Into the soft curves we threw ourselves,
arms and legs spread wide, fearless
in the sparkling cold, deep with delight,
sweeping arcs for angel wings.

Arms and legs spread wide, we
pressed shapes of fearless angels in snow,
sweeping arcs for wings and gowns,
then pulled each other up with mittened hands,

leaving our shapes as angels in the snow.
Careful not to trample our prints,
we pulled each other up by the hand,
proud of the marks we left behind.

Careful not to trample what we left behind
when we were little fearless angels,
Brother, we pulled each other up.

Absolution

1. At first, you clench
   with cold, tighten against it,
   pull your jacket tighter.
   With every step into the white,
   the ground gives
   under your boots.
   You enter the pure:
   untouched expanse,
   white birches, old oaks,
   dry clusters on sumac
   gone from red to brown,
   landscape sketched
   with chalks and charcoal.
   All you have brought here
   weighs heavy on your limbs
   as you trudge, gaze, ache.

2. You walk in cleansing silence,
   a sacredness inherent in weather.
   There is freshness in the cold,
   even if it is difficult
   to breathe it in.
   Your tears,
   whether of sorrow
   or regret,
   or the simple shock
   of meeting winter face to face,
   freeze on your cheeks.
   You slog up hills,
   stomp over prints where
   others have come before,
   tromping down snow
   to make it easier for those
   who will come after,
   your breath ragged,
   puffing small clouds.
   You are not the only one:
   furred coyote scat

next to the trail,
tracks of deer, rabbit, squirrel
in curves and zigzags,
and something even smaller—
mouse? vole?—that dragged
its tail between tiny paws.
Evidence of so much that is
alive, unseen.

3. In time you feel your body
    stoking your own fire
    from the inside.
    You loosen your hold,
    pull off your gloves,
    let your shoulders settle.
    When this kind of day arrives,
    you must enter it,
    take what it bestows.
    You recognize
    your own tracks
    as you come back around.
    Whether earned or given,
    something has released
    as you return
    to where you started.
    You see home now
    through the trees.
    What you carried
    when you set out
    is no longer frozen.
    Through the heat of your
    persistent steps, your belief
    in winter's power,
    it has been transformed
    into invisible vapor
    and released
    into cold blue sky.

All We Can Do Is Name Them
Before They Are Gone Again

At dusk out skiing, Mike glimpses the seven deer
that visit our frozen pond. Anonymous, they materialize,
tromp through drifts, romp in joy across the ice.

More than animals, a mystical phenomenon—
they appear as if conjured. We long to explain
their presence, unexpected as grace. We try

Heart-Toed Dancers. Tawny Curiosity.
Twilight Pursued and Embodied. We almost
know them, Familiar Strangers, as if they are

a Flock of Furred Ancestors Returned,
Noble Knights of Dusk, Antlered Saints,
Monks of the North Woods, The Keepers

of Forest Memories. When we walk deep
amongst the trees, we sometimes feel suddenly
seen and notice one or two standing near,

completely still, Silent Sentries, Hide-
and-Seek Champions, Cunning
Sleight of Hand, They Who Know the Trick

of Invisibility. These Citizens
of the Wooded Alleyways, Always More
Than You Think, Guardian Angels With Hooves

appear like a vision you barely trust,
like in stories we've heard from books or
in church, something holy but alive.

At Home In Every Season, Fierce Survivors,
they have no need of us, though our desire
for them only grows. They Who Will Not Be Studied,

Who Dwell In a Thicket of Quiet,
Pass Through Snow as Through a Veil,
Dissolve to Tracks With No Bodies,

when we blink, they are gone. We miss them
terribly, ache for another glimpse, as if
one day we might finally understand why they come.

Things I Didn't Know I Loved, (Pandemic Edition)

after Nazim Hikmet

It's April 15th, 2020.
I'm sitting at my antique desk—which I
bought when I was spontaneous,
single, at a small-town auction—
by a window with weathered-wood sill.
It's morning, early, the sky blue but
colder than you'd think for such brightness.

I didn't know I loved the cold,
bracing, that forces me to bundle up in sweaters
and wear my wool socks. But I couldn't
bear a world that was always warm,
never a challenge to the animals who burrow
or the humans who close their windows.

I didn't know I loved burrowing animals,
the ones that chew the tulips that have barely
emerged from cold soil. How they ruin
the garden, those scheming rabbits,
those scurrying chipmunks, and find
in my carefully chosen plants all
that they need to eat, to survive, and
multiply, that clever urge.

I didn't know I loved a garden
because my family never had one when
I was a child, only lawns, spreading out
green, monotone, one big flatness, but now
that I am grown I crave variety,
tall perennials with seedy heads
the birds come to sit on, low geraniums,
bell-shaped columbine, all the colors.

I didn't know I loved a wide-green lawn,
(though I don't want one of my own), but
all those summer days of running, tackling,
being tackled by sweat-scented boys,
all those nights of Kick the Can,

scaring ourselves in the dark into wild laughter,
sneaking up to run, kick, scream, rescue
the ones who were caught, waiting
under the porch light to be rescued,
the power of being for one moment a hero,
though it didn't last.   I didn't know
I loved being a hero once.

      I didn't know I loved that dull town
where nothing ever happened, those games
that filled so many hot, humid nights,
those long-gone neighbor kids, rough
and innocent.

      I didn't know I loved innocence,
the plain dark hoodies we wore, the stupid
glass bottles of blackberry brandy raised to our
lips, passed around in a vast cornfield,
the days so long ago that can never be again,
could never be now in the shiny
sophistication of modern adolescence
with their phones and money and thoughtless
privilege.

      I didn't know I loved the past when I
spend so much time looking out this window
planning for the future. I didn't know
I loved windows, the way they divide
me from all that's outside, but are also
transparent, so I can be here and out there
at once, and how, on that long-awaited
spring day, I can open them, let in
the grass-smelling breeze to clear away all
the staleness of cooped-up days, all
the invisible cobwebs I've been ignoring.
How permeable I become
when the sounds of the neighborhood
stream in—a jet overhead, going somewhere,
a child on a bike, a garbage truck doing
what it's meant to do, its workers

more cheery than you'd expect, with their
thick gloves, hopping up onto the side
of the truck for a little ride just partway
down the block to the next set of bins.

    I didn't know I loved garbage trucks
until I wrote these lines. Though three-year-olds
love them more, squeal with excitement when
the big truck drives down the driveway at preschool
beeping backwards, opens like a giant mouth,
picks up the dumpster with robot arms and
lifts it automatically, dumps it with such power,
pouring our trash into its metal belly—how
those little boys laugh with pure
delight. I watch them and every time it
makes me happy. Every time.

    I didn't know I loved watching
children, now that my own are gone
to their own houses, self-sufficient, since
children are my work; but when I can't work,
like now, ordered to stay in my house
that I love (even though it's too small, even
though I want to sell it), maybe more, now,
I miss watching the children, hearing
their loud yells, their irreverent howls
as they climb trees in the woods, poke
with sticks, make potions from mud
and puddle water and acorns and crumpled
wildflower petals, especially now when it's
so silent, I didn't know I loved their noise.
Even though I've lost some of my hearing
from being inside that noise for too many
years, I love it as much as the silence,
which I also love.

    I didn't know I loved the clock
that belonged to my mother and father,
how its pendulum swung in rhythm
for decades and how it now sits on top

of my antique desk still ticking long after
they've died. How I wind it, mindfully,
each week with the golden key and how
old-fashioned it is.   I didn't know
I loved old things until I had to pack up
so many of them in boxes, take them away
to be stored so strangers coming in to see
this old house would be fooled into
perceiving it as more spacious than it is.

       I didn't know I loved the packed-away
things so much. Turns out they are exactly
what I need now that they are inaccessible,
like this day, behind this window,
still closed to the cold blue sky
that I love.

Overheard

Sitting at an Outdoor Table
at the Coffee Shop

Someone is whistling;
I can't tell who.
The air smells like pine needles.
A little girl shuffles down the sidewalk

in new shoes that are too big.
Someone is whistling;
the music floats toward me.
The air smells like pine needles

from an old Christmas tree.
I can't tell who
left it here to dry, drop its needles.
A little girl shuffles down the sidewalk

in no hurry to get anywhere
in new shoes that are too big.
She moves to a rhythm only she can know.
The music floats toward me.

It makes me happy to be here.
The air smells like pine needles,
a green and shuffling music
that someone is whistling.

Called

At four a.m. he rises, startled awake by a gleam of sound.
He slips out wearing just a robe and slippers,
slides open the glass door onto the deck.

Neighbors asleep, shades drawn, lights out.
Snow falls in soft clumps. From just across the pond,
a deep hoot once again echoes in the night

through birches and oaks over to where he stands.
He has never seen its shape, though he scans branches
in the moonless mist. The call haunts him—

a solitary plea, deep silence after. Is it an admission
of loneliness? The great owl waits, as if for a reply,
an answer to its question, sent out into shadows.

He, too, waits. He holds his breath, but tonight
there is no other creature awake besides him and the owl,
or none willing to reveal itself in the dark.

He pulls his robe tighter around his body
against the cold, stands awhile longer, amazed
that something so wild should be so close.

It comes again, piercing the silence, those low
plaintive notes. They resonate deep in his bones,
strike something there—a memory? A premonition?

What has he forgotten that he once knew?
The owl's cry tugs on what's unreachable,
a solitude without words, an unnamed ache.

Then the feathery hush of wings lifting off
and the owl is gone, gliding invisibly
to a place he can't see, can't follow.

He will go back to his warm bed beside his sleeping wife,
try to reenter the ease of dreams.
One night, he is certain, he will catch a glimpse

of that veiled phantom, as if seeing it at last
will solve the mystery of the owl's desire
and perhaps of his own.

In a Harsh Winter, a Relic Appears

Coming upon a stem of lily-of-the-valley,
dried, browning, pressed
between the pages of an old book
of poems, recalls a day

when I took the time to wander
through those quiet York streets and gardens
as if there was nothing more urgent
than breathing, inhaling

the swell of summer, its fragrance
held in these small bells,
perfect embodiment of the newness
that I wait for all through

the bite and false promises
of early spring, its coming at last.
The flowers are pressed next to
a poem called *True Love*,

one I knew well many years ago
but have since forgotten. The lilies,
now dry as ancient paper,
have lost their scent. Yet

their discovery is a surprise gift,
a reminder of a particular kind of day
and how I once knew with certainty
that it would arrive again.

Speaking to Ghosts

Your longing wakes you
before the dawn, light not yet
framing the edges of your window.

In sleep, you called their names;
the sound echoed off stone
right back to you, empty.

You are afraid you've lost
all traces of your dead beloveds.
Either you or they are lost,

but which? In the morning.
you walk through snow,
leave tracks: evidence you are real,

you are here on Earth for a while.
Even when they follow you,
your ghosts leave no marks.

You tell yourself it's all right
to know or not to know,
to speak their names even if

your calls just return to you.
The sound of your own voice
accompanies you home

through the woods,
following only your own tracks.
Perhaps you are not lost after all.

True Religion

In Minnesota, the religion
of the seasons gives us
holy signals
to prepare, to pull
our fur-lined boots
from the back of the closet,
to put up the storm windows.
Changing light,
shortened days, crisp
crumbling smell
of the air tells us
to administer the sacraments:
bake apples, drink cider, scent
everything with cinnamon,
nutmeg, cloves.

It is what we can count on
in a fractious time, when people
are false and bad news
surges like the great flood.
The geese in the pond behind the house
know what's coming:
they squawk without reserve,
ministers announcing
their ritual, gathering here
for a few last days before
the trial of the long flight.
They carry the map
in their hollow bones.

For those of us too heavy
to take flight, wingless
and grounded, yet
unrooted, pacing the surface,
we must find some other saint
to emulate. We look up, seeking
some otherworldly vision.

Perhaps dappled sun
licking leaves
will suffice. We invent
the symbols we need
to reassure us
that we, too, will survive,
that after the freeze,
the turning Earth will
bring us back around.

How did we get our faith
in trees? What convinced us
that the long-awaited
return of spring
was a sacred promise,
would bestow some kind
of salvation?

All we know for sure
is we were plopped,
dazed, into this complexity,
allowed to walk and gaze,
to learn to trust in
its rhythms, its ways.

Easter

What I want to know is
how does the bulb
in darkness of soil
bear that solitude?

So many months of cold
waiting
alone
unaware that it is only one
of dozens of bulbs
planted last fall.

No light reaches down
as cue to changes
that will come.
It must believe the dark
is all there is.

Still, something stirs
in its core one day,
an urge
to push—
undeniable, commanding.

There comes
a specific moment
in the great rhythm
for a root to burst,
a shoot to drive
toward surface.

The bulb is torn,
its familiar shape shattered
by its own longing.

Is it surprised
when its body rises
from below
and meets the light?

Prayer to Become Soil

Even after the storm that rips leaves
from the trees, even as branches crack
and fall, through the empty limbs

the sky remains. Under it, I stand
empty-handed. I pray: make me
into something solid that will last.

Crumble me into soil beneath that sky,
rich, thick, moist. Composed of
what has fallen apart. Humble

enough to embrace the smallest seed.
Help me be modest, quiet, patient
so new roots might push in.

No longer do I want to be the plant,
the flower or fruit. Now is my time
of stillness, to be the dense ground

from which brighter things emerge.
As my blossoming ends, may I become
that which holds what is about to begin.

ACKNOWLEDGMENTS

ffer my gratitude to the journals where some of these poems have
en previously published, sometimes in slightly different versions:

rings	"Litany On An Autumn Late Afternoon"
ollegeville Institute Newsletter)	
at Lakes Review	"Absolution"
erim	"Finality"
in Street Rag	"One of the First Days"
m Egg Review	"Hike To Rattlesnake Ledge"
o Feathers Anthology	"Revision"
stos	"Red"
inge Blossom Review	"Perplexities"
insongs	"Snow Day"
k & Sling	"Lines That Come at One a.m. On the Eve of Trump's Inauguration"
rit First	"Prayer to Become Soil"
king Stick	"In a Harsh Winter, a Relic Appears"
rd Wednesday	"Called"
ter	"Overheard Sitting at an Outdoor Table at the Coffee Shop"
itefish Review	"Lockdown Drill"
consin Review	"Mending"

I am grateful every day for my writing buddies who encoura and inspire me: the Pleasant Avenue writing group, Minneapo Quaker writers, and the children's book writers who have beco dear friends. Special thanks to Lore Roethke and Mary Logue who perceptive comments helped me organize and revise this book. A deep gratitude to my teachers in Hamline University's MFA progra (2002), and the Loft Literary Center Mentor Series mentors a fellow mentees (2009-2010) who boosted my confidence in writing.

My life is richer because of the unconditional friendship of Pe Devenow, hugs from my sweet grandchildren, and the dependa love of my husband Mike Hay. Thank you all for being present.

TITLE INDEX

First Line Index

Printed in the USA
CPSIA information can be obtained
at www.ICGtesting.com
JSHW030117230924
70064JS00006B/19

9 781594 981